VERSES

CHRIS GILL

Collected Poems 2006—2016

Published by PRNTD Publishing 2016

Copyright © Chris Gill 2011

Chris Gill asserts the moral right to
be identified as the author of this work

ISBN 9780994462022

All rights reserved. No part of this book may be
reproduced, stored in a retrieval system, or transmitted
in any form, by any means, including mechanical,
electric, photocopying, recording or otherwise, without the
prior written permission of the publisher.

First published in the United Kingdom in 2011 by
PRNTD Publishing. Republished in Australia in 2016.

www.prntdpublishing.com

For my family

PREFACE

One of the first things that drew me to poetry was how hard it is to actually define. To me, poetry is a way of seeing the world far beyond its literal form. It is a form of art, in the sense that it comments on the world and provokes emotions from within that help us to connect with one another. It's this connection – writer to reader, musician to listener, painter to viewer – that excites me the most. In a world where most connection is made through screens and wires, I think it's essential that literary arts such as poetry are kept alive.

We are all touched by poetry at one stage in our lives, whether it's as obvious as studying prose in our English Literature classes at school, or through the plays we see at the theatre, or even verses sung by our favourite singers. But it's only when we become aware of poetry's metaphysical presence that we begin to notice it everywhere. The graffiti on a bus stop. The conversations we have with interesting strangers. The dreams we have that we try to unravel but simply don't understand. Poetry is everywhere. It's in the air.

This book is my deeply personal, ambiguous yet unabashedly open, fragile yet unafraid letter to the world. It is a collection of poetry, lyrics and stream-of-conscious psychobabble dispensed from the corners of my heart and soul over the past decade[1].

As I shape-shift through each section of this book, journeying from childhood to manhood, it's so gratifying to have a place for all of these weather-worn poems to exist beside one another. Whatever you take from my memoirs and observations, I hope you enjoy reading them as much as I enjoyed freeing them. These are my treasures. These are my scars. These are my verses.

Chris Gill
London, 2011

---

[1] Edited from the original text, for publication in 2016.

PART ONE

CATACOMBS

CHRIS GILL

CATACOMBS

to get here lord
on this day of judgement
i have a story
or two
to tell
every trial and tribulation
every high water and every hell

through every dragon slain
after burning me with their flames
like a piece of timber
until nothing remained
through travelling over burning rocks
after every objection overcome
my journey has just begun

o lord, you must forgive me
i swear i've served my time
i confess before you that i have sinned
danced with the devil once or twice

through every cataclysmic betrayal
that has torn my delicate world apart
i present myself to you fully
i give you the catacombs of my heart

CHRIS GILL

RENDER

sometimes you walk these
weather worn
weary streets
where sirens sing
like bionic birds
and cigarette smoke replaces air
to find solace in anonymity
and a triumph in every tear

you will see the walking dead
with their vacant
menacing expressions
like drones with hate-filled heads
from camden road
down to mornington crescent

and you may render yourself
to these dirty streets
in hope for some retribution
but don't expect much in return
aside from lungs filled with smoke
and pollution

one day you will walk these
weather worn
weary streets
to find you too are one of the
walking dead
you too will find yourself walking
down camden road
like a drone with a hate-filled head
see i came to this city with a hunger
and a pocket full of dreams
now my lungs are weighed down with chemicals
and i have learnt nothing is what it seems

CREASES

you sit there
high upon your corporate throne
you want to straighten out all my creases
every fold
every crinkle
make it even
not a wrinkle

to fit your mould
mild and marketable
make me polished
pristine and profitable
inside your box
silenced and subtle

here i stand
every scribble like a riddle
on my body covered up
they're reading my arms like pages from a book
but they won't explain me
no matter how long they look

he asks: "what is it you want?
how are you willing to get it?"
what he means is: "does your writing have a market?
if so, how are we going to sell it?"
he doesn't listen to my answers
he can barely remember my name
instead he is wondering if my work will create hype
and if i'm willing to play the game

this dirty tube never stops moving
and you can smell the money on their fingertips
but i need all my fingers
to write

when you switch off the lights at night
and you're alone with your thoughts
are you content with this life you lead
and all these shiny things you've bought?

i am an underdog, not a tool
i will be the exception to your rule
i will never be your fucking profit
go rob the soul of some other fool

CHRIS GILL

PENCIL MARKS

bit by bit
i feel things changing
the way i'd dreamt about
for centuries
like photographs of clouds
rearranging
the way i hoped they would
since time began

there you stand
angelic answer to my praying
like a statue
made of stone and silver lining
surrealist fantasy
in all its perfect peculiarity
i feel completed
like ink tattooed on bare flesh

love is blind
yet i can see right inside of you
just one kiss
has got the icebergs melting
like global warmth
you're burning holes through my ozone layer
then peeling back every layer
one by one

bit by bit
i feel things finally shifting
the way i'd read about
in all those wonderful, beautiful books
here you stand
breaki ng ap ar t   my se n te   nc   e   s
yet i feel complete
like ink written over pencil marks

CHRIS GILL

UNDER YOUR WING

so young and naïve
i made you a part of my career
and my dream
i was the first one to believe
all that you told me
but it was not as it seemed

i will never forget the day that we met
i was lost and i was late
and i was dripping with sweat
then you told me something
that i will never forget

you took a chance on me
like no one had before
took me under your wing
with all your stories
champagne
caviar
le grand amour

we attended parties with all the industry's finest
you were always the first one to the bar
you told me that i would be the next big writer
you told me that i would be a star

so when the signs arose that the publication
would be shutting down
i felt the fool and i felt a clown
i will never forget that dismal winter's day
you walked into the office and took my dreams away

i will never forget the day that we met
i was lost and i was late
and i was dripping with sweat
then you told me something
that i will never forget

CHRIS GILL

CLOUDS

for every exit: an entrance
they say
doors do not fight your force
when you push them
words will not simply pack up and leave
when you read them
but you have every ounce of power in you
to remain closed
or to run

the smug smirk slivers though your dream
before you wake
dry mouthed and restless you turn
towards the bright white light
and let your eyes open
it's friday and the day has gone
before you let it begin

will you be making the most of

your oxygen this evening?

will you prepare each word

before it is released?

will you ponder your thoughts like

big

flat

round concepts?

will you find yourself with less and less to prove

and will you keep an eye out for the clues?

all the while you will be dimly aware

this time

that there will be no exception to the rule

and that it is your discretion that will be your tool

two decades have gone by leaving you adjusting

from the impetus of an adolescent project

and you will shift from one

corner of the room to another

unable to really make up your mind

however, despite all of this
and despite of yourself
you notice the record is no longer
skipping in the same way
his words heal like fresh air on your face
and you don't even notice it's now saturday
see, days slip and slide into one another
the way clouds collide
and nothing might change or be gained
but there is truth in those old clichés
and there are lessons to be learnt
in those in-between days

VERSES

CHRIS GILL

PART TWO

ESCAPE TO THE DOCKS

CHRIS GILL

TRAPDOOR MOON

the stars they all came down
like silver snowflakes to the ground
we were left lost and with no sound
the day that you were found

it is only now that we can see
the jewel that was your heart
kept secure inside your corset
guarded deep within your frame
the secrets burnt and buried
beside your name

the stars they all came down
leaving you white as ivory
like cocaine
clothed only in perfect photographs
as you pulled the switch from your brain
and nothing will ever be the same
the day you left us hanging
the whole house was rearranged

it is only now we see
how shipwrecked you had been
my lovely boy, you are adored
could we not have been your lighthouse
guiding you back to shore?

the stars they all came down
like glitter upon a stage
you played othello with such integrity
that it was painfully uncanny
the earth shifted on its axis
and for a moment mother nature died
and the lights came down like the world was a theatre
draping it into darkness and disguise
and you disappeared into the milky moon
that lit up the stage
like you were falling through a trapdoor in the sky

the curtains come down to signify reprise
as you close your eyes and say goodbye
with nothing left to do but try to understand
until we meet again in the promised land

CHRIS GILL

ERA OF HADES

staring into two
spinning almond balls of eye
lampshade skin
blood like wine
arteries pumped with adrenaline
dirty substances
chewed off flesh

skin and bone
stones and sticks
brittle limbs
thorns jagged and stiff
lucifer breathes words through
my hypnotic gaze
and misled ways

grey blood cells bounce
and break
winter wounds
and un-colours me
mummified horizontally
waiting for the great big
coma white
to set me free

dysmorphic days
plagued paragraphs
all over the black-stained sink
there we stood
no common ground aside
from apocalyptic desire

hedonistic hades
before the throne of god
on our four horses
with great big smiles
across our thick cracked skulls

CHRIS GILL

SLEEPING BEAUTY

leaned over my
twenty-first century
new age sleeping beauty
to tuck her in
after one of those wild
up-all-nights
where we just couldn't stay in

you stole my heart like pop art
over synthesised beats and guitars
like audrey had taken a trip to space
to dance with ziggy and the spiders from mars
a mascara made monochrome maze
passed out in your bed sheets for days
a glittery, wine-induced haze
cigarette ash all over the place

we could be heroes
and usually were
my drainpipes and leather
your pearls and your fur
two degenerates
with nothing left
found everything in one another

passed out beside my
twenty-first century
new age sleeping beauty
as the sun rays burn our skin
after one of those wild
up-all-nights
where we just couldn't stay in

CHRIS GILL

BLUR

i have seen that
dazed glaze
over those two naïve eyes
too many times

little sparkly crystals
within your flow of blood
i know exactly how it feels
but none of it is real

parading yourself all over this town
just don't ever forget
what comes up must come down

is this world not beautiful enough as it is?
has nature not handed you enough acrylic
to colour your canvas in?
must you always win?
is your night not finished until you sweat
and you spin?

you think i have lost interest
but i'm just tired of these games
the routine is so familiar now
i know every step and every line
i no longer have the energy
i'm wasting too much time

as i depart the party early
i sober up on my journey back to what i prefer
back before my foreground went out of focus
sending my world into a blur
you remain in ecstasy
but as something i detest
it's finally time to clean up this mess

CHRIS GILL

SOLO

this landscape has changed
foreground still slightly out of focus
but my background now remains
i always knew you'd be the death of me
but i do not feel the same

standing here in parts
unassembled
in knots
waiting for the plot
to unfold

will you paint the scene?
all that sand and sea
come act out this perfect
memory with me
fill the frame
like a photograph once in motion
with all that salty water
and all that salty air
do you dare?

somewhere between

once upon a time

and

happily ever after

we both lost sight of what's important

now i'm standing at the edge alone

of that harbour

watching our little boat

drift solo out to sea

its only passengers:

our memories

CHRIS GILL

ESCAPE TO THE DOCKS

he picked up his dated rucksack
some old worn shoes
to carry him along
several garments like
style-shed skin
a fistful of memories
a few friendships wearing thin

following the moon
like a moth to a lightbulb
he let nature take her course
he let nature go ahead and win
a world was waiting to be changed
a grudge waiting to be erased
he escaped to the docks
like he was running away with the circus

with every bold decision
comes a major transition
but change to him is fuel
pushing him along and holding him up
and fate has nothing to do with luck

so he dropped his clothes and rucksack

to the floor

then let out a

long

rhetoric

sigh…

outside, the dull glow of the summer

fell into the inky ocean

where a large ship cut though the tiny beads

like scissors through a piece of cloth

CHRIS GILL

PART THREE

HOME

CHRIS GILL

ROTARY WASHING LINE

when i was five years old
i used to climb up that rusty old
rotary washing line
like one of those shiny plastic monkeys
from the big bright blue barrel

i would scamper up that metallic pole
like i was
jack climbing up the beanstalk
all the way into my head

no one could get me
way up there
i was safe and i was strong
every time i disappeared
and i could be anywhere
like the indian in the cupboard
or tintin in tibet

if only i could
climb back into my mind
the way i would do as a child
block out all the billboards
banners
and skyscrapers
all the advertisements
halves and quarters

if only i could find a ladder
to climb
instead of selling like a snake
and being sold to like a sponge

every time i step out
underneath that slate-grey sky
it taunts me like an empty page
waiting to be filled with words
sentences and paragraphs
for clouds
punctuation
for birds

CHRIS GILL

every time i walk alone
stuck in the past tense
somewhere lost between
was and will be
i am taunted by my present
and am a slave to my own dreams
waiting for the future to swoop down
come save me

when i was five years old
i used to climb up that rusty old
rotary washing line
like jack climbing up the beanstalk
all the way into my head

until i heard
"fee-fi-fo-fum"
and it would be time for bed

VERSES

CHRIS GILL

HAEGELS HAM

cometh one, cometh all
to ol' haegels ham
the most memorable mark't
in all of the land

once thou hast been
ye ne'er shalt forget
the most peculiar folke
thee ever hath met

cometh one, cometh all
to ol' hamelsham town
where st mary's bells chime
the most unforgettable sound

once thou hast seen
ye shall always know
the secret scars of sussex
that just don't want to let go

cometh one, cometh all
to ol' aylesham town
where different is wrong
and gipsy wears the crown

if thou spent the years
the way i had to do
thou would then understand
ye would then know too

o hailsham, o hailsham
we are finally through

CHRIS GILL

FLICKERS

each memory
moves across my mind
like pictures on a slide show
our bodies intertwined
for several days
that time

the citric seeping
from the juicy orange
into the cracks of my skin
which would sting and sting
more than anything

ferocious chickenpox
my hallucinations and screaming
my mother's hand on my head
reminding me i'm only dreaming

standing in front of that teacher
with the red nose
and acoustic guitar
endlessly trying to recite times tables
but it never wanted to
come out right

riding my bike
without stabilisers
for the very first time
making my father proud
flickers through my mind

each memory
floats across my brain
like ghosts drifting through an old house
our bodies both combined
for several days
that time

CHRIS GILL

HOME

large white houses like
the ones out of a design magazine
you pass
visions of purity and nuclear bliss
laughter and music
a mother's kiss

the street meanders like a river
the air polluted with the odour
of a plant
three more steps
staircase situated slumped
foaming mouth
sullen eyes
the worst surprise

twenty two years pass
and never do you arrive home
to a man with such darkness in his eyes
come to warn you of your
imaginary invincibility

chills creep up across your neck
like tiny cat paws
like a tiny mouse
racing up your tiny staircase

yet all you were trying to do
was trying to make a home
all you were trying to do
was trying to find somewhere to call your own

you could be content and complete
in one place
laughter and music
your mother's kiss…

it's just not this

CHRIS GILL

PART FOUR

WIRES

CHRIS GILL

SHINY COINS

it's a virtual hollywood boulevard
spat out as the century shifts
faces gaunt and glossy
skin hangs and sags against bird-like skulls
empty eyes gaze into the electronic bulb's
reflection
mirrors. masquerades. deception.

page after page of people products
listlessly sold to the thought police
conditioned and contained
to be intertwined and defaced
stored and remade
in this global database

the boy with silver hair
has nothing at all to say
so he sits perched upon his ledge
like a bird upon a billboard
drawing so much interest and awe
as originality is running thin
where is the next one of a kind
what is the next big thing?

colour fades
as a bolder yearning invades
every exclusive, collective party loses its appeal
for something more real
the stars become tiny shiny coins
and the sky a colossal vending machine above us
our bodies become cornfields brushing side to side
in the ever-shifting seasonal snake of existence
in which we are enslaved to persistence

it is in this perfect place of purgatory
i decide to leave your world behind
a picture paints a thousand lies

CHRIS GILL

ODE TO PLANET EARTH

one thing i will never understand
is the careless
thoughtless ways of man
like all that land and sea and sand
belongs within his greedy hands

nature is not here to serve us
it is not ours to destroy
we need to take care of this island
a greater consciousness we need to employ
we must learn to reuse plastic
so our children's children too can enjoy
this world and all its beauty
planet earth is not a toy

nature is not ours to claim we own
we must respect this rock we call our home
we must leave this island in a recovered state
before it really finally is too late
it is for each of us, both you and i
to make a difference until the day we die

VERSES

CHRIS GILL

WIRES

we sit in lines
wires connecting one another
like reconstructed veins
mouths and ears like
perfect circular holes
keeping us joined together
in a circuit
like a gigantic electric switchboard

like programmed plants
we sit opposite one another
like an assortment of switches and parts
flashing lights and noisy modems
are now more essential than hearts
wired into one another
it's so hard to feel a thing
we may even eventually begin
to wake up and wonder:
when will it be time to disconnect?
pull out all the different coloured cords
that made us forget

it's like a non-stop social spinning wheel
of superficial self-identity
where nothing is real
when all you see and hear is static
it's so hard to figure out
what you really feel

of course this entire mechanical maze
is just deceptive and distractive
to keep us hypnotised and in a haze
to hinder our inquisitive
human nature
to not quench our thirst for justice
but instead remove it altogether
burn off our taste buds when we are sleeping
one
by
one
so remember remember
the leaks of december

how seeing the truth felt like heaven
on our virgin eyes
course, it's so easy to forget
when we're force fed fabricated fodder
feature after feature
lie after lie
this is what murdoch meant
this is your beloved government

so those who try to expose
know
they will end up caged like an animal
beaten bruised and buried
stripped naked in front of millions
televised in front of brainwashed civilians
google has got you gagged
and facebook has got your facts
keep smiling slave
they have your brain
so just keep tweeting and relax

and more bad news piles in
every time i switch that damn thing on
micro melancholy makes me mute
and leaves me with such little hope
with barely a single suggestion
just compilations of complaints
that earthquake over there
is going to shake and shake me
until i just don't care
shake me to the grave
and leave my bones completely bare

lately i been having these
same old twisted dreams
and i been bombarded by big broad billboards
filled with tits and fake bright white beams
and i see this same old spellbound stare
in every carbon copy store
people stepping over other people
to purchase pretty products and then want more
it's enough to leave you hollow
leave you rotten to the core

every hipster fashion magazine
wants me hysterical and hexagon
wants me polished dazed and confused
ready to fold up and reuse
ready to disguise and eject my debate
wants me gutted gassed and gaffer-taped
wants me remade 'right' and raw and raped

let me age like
i'm supposed to
with great big lines
across my face
indicating endless
fits of laughter
and countless rounds
of frowns

don't sell me a world
thought up by another's mind
don't reconstruct my veins with wires
my own soul i need to find
let my mind run free like a child

so my creativity i can use
let me bend all these straight lines
and right angles
into a shape that personally
i can choose

come join me in my controversial project
to rise up
protest and protect
against the machine and the machines
let us all finally disconnect
the time is now to pull the plugs
right out of our brains and eyes
take back our souls and minds
it's the only way we will truly know
ready:
three
two
one
let's go…

CHRIS GILL

PART FIVE

ORACLES UNDER CITY LIGHTS

CHRIS GILL

ORACLES

as sirens chant mantras of divinity
fluorescent signs illuminate the sky
every street corner is filled with sūtras
like oracles under city lights
i chased the neon like an ambitious bull
to a blood-red rag
only to find that when i reached these dreams
of 'so-called'
my world was plunged into pitch black

i learnt the light radiates from within
like a galaxy wrapped around a sun
i found nirvāṇa amidst rush hour
oṃ maṇi padme hūṃ
step forward into the noise
to find an inner silence
step forward to find peace
while immersing yourself
within violence

this is a rebirth
a beginning
true enlightenment
face first on the pavement
outside the open-all-night
convenience store

CHRIS GILL

GENIE

they're trying to
commercialise me
like extracting a genie
from a lamp
they're trying to
water down my words
lessen my language
it's absurd
polluted with precision
tightening up
my cogs
sprinkling me with
social strategies
chopping down my sentences
like logs

how long must we defend our craft
before they understand?
how many times must we explain our art
before he says we can?
creation cannot be easily defined
with data on a grid
emotions provide us with so much more
than number-crunching could ever give

still you won't give in
until you see our creative demise
still you won't let up
until my engine's been utterly optimised

CHRIS GILL

VHS

i could count the times
on one hand that we
rendezvoused
since i was rejected
like an old vhs tape from the recorder
i could count the times
i jumped on an old red bus
to make it to your side of town
except it's like pulling teeth
from rotten gums
like pulling shards
from a structured heart
reflections of a time when
i was all mine
no contract to a telephone provider
no pay check from an employer
littering my letterbox
these little reminders
like the time you
threw me a red herring
but it just became
my red letter year

VERSES

CHRIS GILL

AN ALTERNATE VISION

"it's a new dawn
it's a new day"
blasts through these speakers
like bright light
through a black net
doom and gloom
print the papers
like this as good
as it's gon' get
yet
"…i'm feeling gooood"
see
this year gon' be a good one
i can feel it in my bones
as we occupy the internet
protest to protect our homes
the word's in from new orleans
like a jazz player's favourite song
we are the 99%
so which side are you on?

this year let's all be activists
take our signs and make marching a trend
fight big government and corporations
that turn a profit every time we spend
let's no longer just be consumers
let's be people with wisdom too
let's march until we lose our voices
until our fists are black and blue

this year let's all be feminists
the fight's not just for women
but men too
to put out the flames of patriarchy finally
until we're all equal
him, her
me and you

CHRIS GILL

this year let's all be environmentalists
to realise nature's not our possession
we need to take better care of the planet
make the blue marble our new obsession
this new year, twenty-twelve
is filled with hope and reconnection
let's show each other love
respect and true affection
at the bottom of the rainbow
a pot of freedom is what i see
i see sunshine and blue skies
through the pohutukawa and palm trees

let's join forces and make a promise
to from now on make informed decisions
in return i'll make a vow
to keep on writing with
an alternate vision

VERSES

CHRIS GILL

CAMDEN TOWN

those

dusty old streets

cigarette ash

in my hair

whiskey and wine

in the air

folk

harder than rock

sirens seeping

soaring past

that murky old lock

i was just

an angry young man

back then

so much to prove

as i darted through

worries weighing down

my mind

back then

ambitions turning me blind

as i hurried towards the tube

that
welcoming old bar
with its jazz band
new orleans
vibe
old drunks
homes along the pavement
like algae
along the seabed

i was just
a determined young man
back then
with so much to get
off my chest
trying to learn from
each experience
seeing life as just
one big test
that concrete old flat
with its revolving rooms
that friendly old woman
singing that same old tune
she's since passed on
finally left north london

i'll soon be
an enlightened old man
with nothing
left to prove
but i will never forget
coming up
just trying to
make the world move

oh, camden town
where would i be without you?

VERSES

CHRIS GILL

SPINE

a chest opened wide like the centre of a book
words like organs spilled onto the floor
nothing was left but the twisted old spine

VERSES

CHRIS GILL

NOSTALGIA

on this eager quest
to become something epic
something along the way
completely changed
now i don't recognise you
or my face

where did those days go
where it all felt so simple
like a broken jukebox
that song is stuck on repeat
within my mind
like a precious memory
frozen in time

nostalgia seeps in
like the winter chill in the night
like grey skies overhead
like rotten marrow in my bones

where did those summers go
spent carefree and outdoors?
the gift of foresight
makes these memories unflawed
makes them heavenly
like a filter is glazed
over every single one of them

on this eager quest
to find something epic
something completely shifted
along the way
like a light being switched on
in a pitch black room

my chest opened wide like the centre of a book
my words like organs spilled onto the floor
nothing was left but my twisted old spine
and my face wasn't mine

as i step forward clutching my past
like a skeleton key
i close my eyes and unlock the door
directly in front of me
i take my first step forward
into the bright white lights of the unknown

i open my eyes

VERSES

CHRIS GILL

PART SIX

THE OTHER SIDE

CHRIS GILL

FORWARD

sometimes to move forward
you have to go back
revisit all those paths you've tread
remember what was in your head

VERSES

CHRIS GILL

THE OTHER SIDE

had to move a few mountains
burn a few bridges
exorcise a few ghosts
cross a few oceans
to begin letting go
learn the art of forgiveness

i'll see you there
on the other side
where the darkness meets the light
where the turning of the tides
finally resides

i called out to you
in the darkness of the night
where the thames meets the tasman
where your blood meets my veins

i'll see you there
on the other side
where we transcend this lifetime
and where the next one
has already begun

i'll see you there

CHRIS GILL

BRANCHES

as the branches fall
off our family tree
one by one
the mysteries of my heritage
get lost in the murky rivers
of history

this thing passed down
through my genes
stops me from standing tall
speaking up
keeps me in panic
wide awake

if i could go back
and do the last decade again
what would i change?
if i just keep climbing up this rock
will it be lonely at the top?

as the last branches fall
from our family tree
soon all will be left is you
and is me

CHRIS GILL

MORNING GLOW

the haze
opens up another day
those burning rays
have something to say
all those sewer rats
ready to feast on decay
teeth chatter
skin perspires
the scent of money
on everybody's fingertips
blind moles searching
through the darkness
ready to take home
what they think they deserve

the crimson dusk
closes another day
those twinkling stars
have something to say
all those cockroaches
waiting to be paid

VERSES

CHRIS GILL

THE STOLEN STREETS

the noise of the chattering train
envelopes itself within
the haunted humming heartbeat
of the dusty pavements of redfern
the stolen streets

the glistening harbours
with their inky blues
are trodden on by endless wanderers
in designer shoes
are built on mountains of bones

the red red heart
of this red red land
was eternally broken
by the white white man
when he came and stole it

the noise of the crying woman
is drowned out by sirens
and the smashing of the auction hammer
as they place bids over her land
as i place bids over her land

the beautiful sandy beaches
with their powerfully ruthless waves
gave way to the four horsemen of the apocalypse
ready to turn the people into slaves
strip them of their origins

these streets are not my own
underneath are not my bones
this stolen land is not my home

CHRIS GILL

OTHER

i've got a compass in my hand
although my heart bleeds for my home planet
i see this world through alien eyes
it simply makes no sense to me
i hear your words as jagged sounds
i just follow the tone of your voice
even though your language makes no sense to me
you simply make no sense to me

i am other
another kind
fell from a star
from far away
sent to deliver one simple message:

the road is long
but this life is short
don't give in and don't give up
don't let your possessions possess you
know that all there really is
is love

see, our worlds are not that different
beyond the different air and terrain
our species are not so far apart
underneath we're one and the same
you've got a compass in your hand
your heart bleeds because it's been broken
my words sound to you like jagged sounds
though i haven't yet spoken

you are other
another kind
from this strange, strange world
so far away
and you've taught me one simple lesson:

the road is long
but this life is short
don't give in and don't give up
don't let your obsessions overtake you
know that all there truly is
is love

and you are loved

CHRIS GILL

WAVES

let the waves
break around you
invite the salt in
allow the tide to
wrap around you
like a blanket
then disappear
into its darkest depths

this is the cycle of life

VERSES

CHRIS GILL

TRIGGERS

like a broken old record player
stuck on playing the blues
these memories are so familiar
like a worn-out pair of shoes

when we were youthful
life seemed so long
it all felt so possible
oh, how we were wrong

so young and ambitious
with everything ahead
life was one big party
getting out of our heads

like a black and white movie
with every line memorised
those faces are so familiar
like they're frozen in time

so young and determined
can't say we didn't try
so spontaneous and reckless
these memories are mummified

when we were youthful
life seemed so long
it all seemed so important
oh, how we were wrong
my god, we were so wrong

train rides along the chalky coast
remind me of that distant world
remind me that we were all really there
that we all really existed

little triggers bring back the songs we'd sing
nostalgia's such a dangerous thing

CHRIS GILL

SCATTERED

withered and worn hands
just like yours were
before you left us
in november
withered and worn hands
that's what mine will be
when i look back at my life
reflecting on how it's been

wondering where the time went
whether i made enough wealth
wondering whether i saw enough
whether i did enough to help
wondering if i was destined
to be a walking contradiction
for a life of unfulfilled dreams
unread prose and fiction

withered and worn hands
that's how mine will be
just like yours were that november
before you were scattered into the sea

those hands
worn out but strong
from scrubbing out
the hardest stains
covered in creases
from the eras you survived

those hands
that once held the hands
of the one you loved
before he was taken away
like all the others you lost
they once carried my mother
they once carried me
they once carried my sister
now they're lost at sea

those hands
squeezed juice from the grapefruits
that grew from our family tree
before handing it over
like all the lessons you taught me

now you're finally free

CHRIS GILL

PARADISE

ready to close the chapter
of the last ten years
a decade of decadence

sometimes to move forward
you have to go back
revisit all those paths you've tread
remember what was in your head
sometimes it takes a while
to start to feel nice
sometimes it takes a while
to find your paradise

but here i lay
beneath the blistering sun
listening to the kookaburras
the next chapter's already begun

see, life moves in circles
glides along symmetrically
now i've recoiled
repainted my memories
my pain turned out to be
my pleasure so pure
while your poison turned out
to be my cure

i lay down beneath
the peeling gum trees
let the crickets crawl all over me

and i feel exactly where
i'm supposed to be

CHRIS GILL

AFTERTHOUGHT

we face each other
like two mirrors
no end point
no final ground
a story left untold
a riddle left unsolved
an infinite paradox

meanwhile i find myself
stuck outside an hour glass looking in
watching the sand pour down
and my time run thin

ABOUT THE AUTHOR

Chris Gill spent time growing up in both England and New Zealand, studied journalism at university in Hampshire and worked as a copywriter in London. He released his dystopian debut novel through his co-founded publishing company, PRNTD, in 2015. He now lives in Sydney, Australia.

Twitter @ChrisWGill

www.chrisgillbooks.com

www.ingramcontent.com/pod-product-compliance
Lightning Source LLC
Chambersburg PA
CBHW020620300426
44113CB00007B/716